MW00768741

After Seventy Years in Babylon

This is what the LORD says: *"When seventy years are completed for Babylon, I will come to you and fulfill my good promise to bring you back to this place."*
Jeremiah 29:10 (NIV)

Published by Blue Dragon Publishing,LLC.

www.blue-dragon-publishing.com

ISBN 978-1-939696-20-5 (hardbound)

ISBN 978-1-939696-21-2 (paperback)

Library of Congress Control Number: 2017956018

Cover illustration by Olympia Ghosh "River of Living Water"

REL012020 Religion/Christian Life/Women's Issues

REL012130 Religion/Christian Life/Devotional

REL012010 Religion/Christian Life/Death, Grief, Bereavement

Printed in the U.S.A.

 Blue Dragon Publishing

Dedication

I dedicate this book to my husband who always encourages me, prays for me, and helps me meet my goals. And to my daughter, who took my words and, to my thrilled amazement, turned them into a real book.

For the Upper Room Chapter of the
Daughters of the Holy Cross

A special thanks to Adelaide Beall, Shirley Hauser, and Virginia Smith, all members of the Upper Room Chapter of the Daughters of the Holy Cross, who contributed devotional thoughts to this book.

Jesus said, *"I am the vine; you are the branches. Whoever abides in me and I in him, he it is that bears much fruit, for apart from me you can do nothing."*
John 15:5

Contents

Preface

The readings in *After Seventy Years in Babylon* are intended to help seniors who are experiencing challenges primarily associated with growing older. The book contains devotionals written from a Christian perspective with help from sisters in the Lord. Each of us is approaching, or are currently in, our senior years. It also contains selected hymns, readings, and prayers intended to encourage.

Age-related challenges are real and may seem overwhelming, even frightening at times; but He has promised, *"...I, the Lord your God, hold your right hand; it is I who say to you, 'Fear not, I am the one who helps you'"* (Isaiah 41:13).

God has expectations for our lives. There is no time to be depressed about age, to be frozen by apprehension, or to race around trying not to think about it. The author of Hebrews tells us, *"We want each of you to show the same diligence to the very end, so that what you hope for may be fully realized. We do not want you to be lazy, but to imitate those who through faith and patience inherit what has been promised"* (6:11-12, NKJV).

So this little book is presented to you in the hope that your joy, your peace, and your confidence in God will be increased. Scripture tells us *"...God will supply every need of yours according to his riches in glory in Christ Jesus"* (Philippians 4:19).

Changing Appearance

I thought my mother was beautiful in her later years, but she used to say, "I wake up feeling just like I always have, then I walk by a mirror and think, 'Who is that old woman?'" Now I get it. It's strange to watch yourself change. Not long ago my grandson found a picture of me at eighteen, and with a shocked look said, "Is that you, Gramma?"

We live in a world that sets an unrealistic standard for females of all ages. I certainly worried when my lovely, young daughter was so distressed over every pound and every pimple. Many terrified mothers have struggled trying to find help to save an anorexic daughter's life.

Paul warns us, "Don't copy the behavior and customs of this world, but let God transform you into a new person by changing the way you think. Then you will learn to know God's will for you, which is good and pleasing and perfect" (Romans 12:2, NLT).

The Message provides an interesting paraphrase of Romans 12:2: *"Don't become so well-adjusted to your culture that you fit into it without even thinking."*

We find in the Bible a description of the coming Messiah: *"He had no form or majesty that we should look at Him, and no beauty that we should desire Him"* (Isaiah 53:2b).

Why wouldn't Jesus have been the most handsome man who ever lived? He was to God. *"For the Lord sees not as man sees: man looks on the outward appearance, but the Lord looks on the heart"* (I Samuel 16:7b).

Preceding Prayer

The prayer preceding all prayer is, "may it be the real I who speaks. May it be the real Thou that I speak to." [i]

- C.S. Lewis

Prayer

Lord, change my thinking, so that my priority is to be beautiful to you, as you look at my heart.

Gray Hair

My husband has no gray hair. You may think that isn't unusual; but, we have been married 49 years, and we weren't particularly young when we married. Like my mother, I am almost totally gray. My hubby swears he really likes my hair. "Please don't change it," he says. (I wonder if he is trying to save money spent at the salon.) Nevertheless, the first time someone thinks I am his mother, I am on my way for color and highlights.

Growing older may bring many challenges. Sometimes we become afraid and want to cry out to God, as the Psalmist did, *"So even to old age and gray hairs, O God, do not forsake me"* (Psalm 71:18).

Praise God! He gives us a promise specifically for seniors: *"Even to your old age and gray hairs I am He, I am He who will sustain you. I have made you and I will carry you; I will sustain you and I will rescue you"* (Isaiah 46:4, NIV). He made, carries, sustains, and rescues us because he loves us, and his love continues through this life and into eternity.

In his book *Knowing God,* J.I. Packer describes the significance of the love of God in the life of a believer: "Thus, so far as we are concerned, God is love to us—holy, omnipotent love—at every moment and in every event of every day's life. Even when we cannot see the why and the wherefore of God's dealings, we know that there is love in and behind them, and so we can rejoice always, even when, humanly speaking, things are going wrong. We know that the true story of our life, when known, will prove to be, as the hymn says 'mercy from first to last'-and we are content." ᵢᵢ

> The steadfast love of the Lord never ceases; His mercies never come to an end; they are new every morning; great is your faithfulness.
> "The Lord is my portion," says my soul, "therefore I will hope in him."
> The Lord is good to those who wait for Him, to the soul who seeks Him.
> It is good that one should wait quietly for the salvation of the Lord.
>
> Lamentations 3:22-26

Prayer

Father God, thank You for Your eternal love, and Your promise to carry me and sustain me whatever my need.

Accidents

I'll bet I have fallen hundreds of times. Always busy, hurried, and a little absent-minded (my sister called me scatterbrained), I rush on until a fall causes a sudden stop. A sprained ankle when I was fifteen was the first, and one of very few injuries which required medical attention greater than an antibiotic cream and a band-aid.

About seven months ago, I fell flat on my face in my sister's foyer. It scared her so badly she didn't stop to call me "scatterbrained" or anything. She just ran for ice.

I broke my nose, my maxillary bone, and my right arm in two places. Strangely, I had no awareness of falling until my face hit the floor.

Every test known to my doctor was done to determine why I fell. Scary-sounding test results proved not to be a problem, and the doctors still have no idea why I fell. The whole thing was alarming to me. Why did it happen? Was another serious fall just around the corner? I had a crisis of confidence.

God's word reminds, *"...do not be surprised at the fiery trial when it comes upon you to test you, as though something strange were happening to you..."* (I Peter 4:12-13). Difficulties—trips, falls, and broken things—are a part of life. What a blessing if we have lived lives that are surprised by painful happenings.

Paul's counsels, *"Be joyful in hope, patient in affliction, and faithful in prayer"* (Romans 12:12 NIV). Sometimes I forget that running to the Lord is the quickest way back to confidence and joy. *"Come and let us return to the Lord; for He has torn, but He will heal us; He has stricken, but He will bind us up"* (Hosea 6:1, NKJV).

He is always there, *"God is our refuge and strength, a very present help in trouble"* (Psalm 46:1). *"And who is a Rock except our God"* (Psalm 18:31b).

Prayer

*Holy Spirit, draw my attention quickly to the
Father, when I find myself surprised and
bewildered by accidents and pain. In Him I will
find peace, and my joy will be renewed.*

Downsizing

About ten years ago, we moved from a roomy house with lots of storage into a studio apartment and an RV. It took a while. My husband said I stared at each item for ten minutes. He exaggerates. But I admit that I was attempting to see the future. What might I need some day? Mostly, I treasured my possessions.

I managed finally to get through the clean out, the give-away, and the garage sale. I kept only the items we actually needed and a few of the items that triggered special memories. It was amazingly liberating to let go of so much stuff. I guess I did sort of cheat by letting my adult offspring choose and take items special to them. I get to visit those things in their homes. (I vow to myself that I will not check to see that the things are still there through the years. It's none of my business, and no measure of their love for me, whether they keep the things or not.)

Jesus warned, *"Do not lay up for yourselves treasures on earth, where moth and rust destroy and where thieves break in and steal: but lay up for yourselves treasures in heaven, where neither moth nor rust destroys and where thieves do not break in and steal. For where your treasure is, there your heart will be also"* (Matthew 6:19-21).

We sold the RV a few years ago. We now have a two-bedroom place with more storage. The rooms and the closets are full again, but I hope not overly full. I try not to hold on to material things too tightly.

Someone may need those things I am keeping but not using.

My favorite consignment store handles auctions. I get their emails with the auction previews. Large houses, full of stuff, and all of it for sale. Someone has collected all that stuff. They have no children or their children don't want their collection. Maybe the heirs have no room, or they need the money. But, the delusive nature of hording worldly treasures is apparent. *"I cried out to you, O Lord: I say 'you are my refuge, my portion in the land of the living'"* (Psalm 142:5).

Prayer

*Help me, Lord, to always choose You as my
portion in the land.*

True Charity

I do not believe that one can settle how much we should give. I am afraid the only safe rule is to give more than we can spare. In other words, if our expenditure on comforts, luxuries, amusements, etc., is up to the standard common among those with the same income as our own, we are probably giving away too little. If our charities do not at all pinch or hamper us, I should say they are too small. There ought to be things we should like to do and cannot do because our charities expenditure excludes them. [iii]

C.S. Lewis

Loss of a Child

The loss of a child must be one of life's worst experiences. When my grandmother lost a middle-aged daughter, I watched her grieve and frequently heard her say, "Your children aren't supposed to die before you."

When my brother was killed in an automobile accident at the age of twenty-three, I wondered if my mother would ever get over it. In her grief, Mom cried; she was angry, and she refused to believe he was dead. She seemed lost for days, and so sad for months. It was years before her memories brought laughter instead of pain.

God understands that kind of pain: The Psalmist said: *"Have mercy on me, O Lord, for I am in trouble; my eye wastes away with grief, yes, my soul and my body! For my life is spent with grief, and my years with sighing..."* (Psalm 31:9-10a, NKJV). The pain of the loss of his children must have been more of Job's agony than his boils.

An Anglican Prayer Book reminds us, *"In the midst of life, we are in death; whom may we seek as our helper, but You, O Lord..."*[iv]

"As a father shows compassion to his children, so the Lord shows compassion on those who fear Him. For He knows our frame; He remembers that we are dust. As for man, his days are like grass, he flourishes like a flower of the field; for the wind passes over it, and it is gone, and its place knows it

no more. But the steadfast love of the Lord is from everlasting to everlasting on those who fear Him, and His righteousness to children's children" (Psalm 103: 15-17).

Prayer

O God, who's most dear Son did take little children into His arms and bless them; Give us grace we beseech thee, to entrust the soul of this thy child to thy never-failing care and love, and to bring us all to thy heavenly kingdom; through the same, thy Son, Jesus Christ our Lord. Amen.

    - From the Book of Common Prayer

Wits End

"Life can be like a ship rolling in the midst of a stormy sea: up one second reaching for the stars, the next second plummeting to the depths." [vi] The Psalmist wrote of those who went out on the sea in ships, *"They reeled and staggered like drunken men; they were at their wits end"* (Psalm 107:27).

Last night, after laughing and enjoying stories about an extraordinary family trip, we learned that a new symptom had appeared in a loved one who we thought was free and clear of cancer. Fasten your life-vest!

Jesus and some of his disciples got into a boat. *"...suddenly a great tempest arose on the sea, so that the boat was covered with waves. But He was asleep. Then His disciples came to Him and awoke Him saying, 'Lord, save us! We are perishing!' But He said to them, 'Why are you fearful, O you of little faith?' Then He arose and rebuked the winds and the sea, and there was a great calm"* (Matthew 8:24-26, NKJV).

The Lord will not fail us when we reach our personal wits end. *"Then they cried to the Lord in their trouble, and He delivered them from their distresses"* (Psalm 107:28).

Prayer

Lord, calm the raging sea of my mind. Build my faith. Give us all Your peace as we pray, watch, and wait.

Rhyme or Reason

Something comes out of nowhere. It is unexpected. There is no apparent reason. No positive outcome can be imagined.

"There's no rhyme or reason. Why did they do that? Why did that happen?" I cry.

Some in their confusion might add, "God only knows," and with that affirmation, they are closer to the truth.

There is wisdom that God shares with His children, and there is wisdom that belongs only to God.

I have felt ashamed and guilty when, in times of difficulty, I have found myself more depressed or distressed than I thought a Christian should be. Worse, I have judged others for not meeting my personal definition of serene spirituality. Such attitudes, Packer writes, arise when we believe we receive God's providential wisdom as we grow spiritually.[vii] My idea that I (or others), if spiritual enough, would understand all God's ways, is absurd.

To meet my God-given responsibilities, God shares the wisdom I need, to do what He has given me to do. Bible characters and their choices teach me what is and isn't wise behavior. The book of Proverbs is full of Godly wisdom. Additionally, the Holy Spirit directs my life to teach me, to change me, and to train me. But God has not promised that I will understand all that befalls me.

I am thankful for the scriptures and the discernment God gives, and I must always be cautious of my human tendencies. According to Packer, "Our intelligence and cleverness must be harnessed to a right end. Wisdom [God shares with His children] is the power to see, and the inclination to choose, the best and highest goals, together with the surest means of attainment. Wisdom is in fact, the practical side of moral goodness." [viii]

I am also thankful that providential wisdom is not in my domain. It is good that it belongs only to God.

Prayer

Lord, thank You for giving me a place to be and work to do. Thank You for making the wisdom I need available to me. Help me to receive from Your hand, all those things You will show me that I need, and I presently cannot understand.

I Am Not Skilled to Understand

I am not skilled to understand
What God hath willed, what God hath planned;
I only know at His right hand
Stands One who is my Savior.

I take Him at His word and deed:
"Christ died to save me," this I read;
And in my heart I find a need of
One who is my Savior.

That He should leave His place on high
And come for sinful man to die,
You count it strange? So once did I,
Before I knew my Savior.

Yes, living, dying, let me bring
My strength, my solace, from this spring,
That He who lives to be my King
Once died to be my Savior!

Dora Greenwell
(1821-1882)

Anxiety and Sleeplessness

My mind began to race as soon as I laid my head on the pillow. It had become an expected nightly routine, like brushing my teeth. I was disturbingly anxious and too often a sleepless person. My continued exhaustion made me irritable, impatient, and nervous. Yet, scripture tells us that God gives His children sleep. *"It is vain for you to rise up early, to sit up late, to eat the bread of sorrows; for so He gives His beloved sleep"* (Psalm 127:2, NKJV).

Paul tells us not to be anxious: *"Do not be anxious about anything, but in everything, by prayer and supplication, with thanksgiving let your request be known to God. And the peace of God, which surpasses all understanding, will guard your hearts and minds through Christ Jesus"* (Philippians 4:6-7).

Though many things may cause sleeplessness, God led me to replace computer solitaire with Bible study and prayer on sleepless nights. He also showed me that my mind was too filled with worldly things. Violent TV and movies, crude comedies, and many of the news programs had to go. *"All things are lawful for me, but not all things are helpful"* (I Corinthians 6:12).

The Holy Spirit could hardly get my attention. *"For to be carnally minded is death, but to be spiritually minded is life and peace"* (Romans 8:6, NKJV).

Prayer

Lord, help me avoid filling my mind with worldly noises and fears. Give me a quiet mind that is able to meditate on you and your word.

The Anglican Prayer Book says it well: "Lord God, You who knows our every weakness, put away from us all worry and every anxious fear. Having ended the work and play of this day under Your care and protection, we now commit ourselves, and all whom we love, into Your gracious keeping; and as night comes, provide for us, we pray, Your priceless gift of sleep; through Jesus Christ our Lord. Amen."[ix]

Forgetfulness

Funny emails about forgetfulness get passed around online continuously. They make us laugh as we hide our fears, and jokingly relate to the absentmindedness of the comic characters who forget. Alzheimer's disease has probably taken the place of cancer as the most feared disease. It is dreaded more than death by many.

How do we face the possibility of having that awful disease? Jesus said, *"Therefore do not worry about tomorrow, for tomorrow will worry about its own things. Sufficient for today is its own trouble"* (Matthew 6:34, NKJV). And He said, *"Can any of you by being anxious add a single hour to his span of life?"* (Matthew 6:27).

When we lose the keys or forget why we turned the computer on, the temptation to worry is still strong.

Still Alice, the recent movie about Alzheimer's disease, shows Alice writing out directions for herself for committing suicide and placing reminders around the house. Choosing a different path, I intend to leave lots of reminders about my intention to remember God when my days of forgetfulness come. There isn't a scriptural reason to believe that the Holy Spirit will not be with me during my entire life on earth; or to believe that the Holy Spirit will forget God the Father or Jesus.

My prayer is that with a grateful heart, these verses will be in my mind a long time: *"Bless the Lord, O my soul and forget not His benefits"* (Psalm 103:2); *"Remember the wondrous works that He has done"* (I Chronicles 16:12); and, *"When my life was fainting away, I remembered the Lord..."* (Jonah 2:7).

Further, my request to my family will be: Don't let me sit in front of a TV every day. Keep me busy doing helpful things; let me hear lots of scripture and my favorite hymns; help me partake of the bread and wine as long as possible.

And even if I am no longer able to do those things, I believe the Holy Spirit will help me know, deep in my soul, that God remembers me, for He said, *"Can a woman forget her nursing child, that she should have no compassion on the son of her womb? Even these may forget, yet I will not forget you. I have engraved you on the palms of my hands"* (Isaiah 49:15-16a).

Prayer

Lord, grant me the faith to trust You totally.

Death

"For you died, and your life is hidden with Christ in God. When Christ who is our life appears, then you also will appear with Him in glory."
                                                    Colossians 3:3-4

My dear friend Adelaide Beall and I discussed death. She told me that she asked the Lord to explain to her about death, dying, and losing.

Jesus, so kind and patient, always ready to answer, replied to her. "Death is letting go—giving up—turning loose: It is letting go of having your own way; letting go of knowing how things should be; losing control over others and situations; dying to self. Death is giving up judging others, criticizing, or gossiping. In this death, there is freedom. Freedom to love. Freedom to accept others as they are. My job, child, is to bring about change in their hearts. Your job is to lose the ideas the world has given and simply love. In death, there is joy and abundant life. Die to self and live in Me."

Oh, Lord, I want to, I truly do. But, even this I cannot do without Your help and grace. Be constantly by my side and in my life, teaching me how to die, so I can live in You and through You. Teach me the joy of surrender—of losing.

Prayer

*Dear Father, walk with me to the cross, the one
You have given me to carry. Hold my hand as I
make my way and as I kneel for it to be placed on
my back as Jesus did. Help me to surrender to
Your will. Help me to believe You. Help my
unbelief. Help me to experience in my surrender
that Your yoke is easy, and Your burden is light.
Show me that You will never give a task that is
greater than I can bear. Show me that all You
desire from me is me. Show me that You desire to
give me a life eternally connected to You.*

Encouragement

"So we do not lose heart. Though our outer self is wasting away, our inner self is being renewed day by day. For this light, momentary affliction is preparing for us an eternal weight of glory beyond all comparison as we look not at the things that are seen, but to the things that are unseen. For the things which are seen are transient, but the things that are unseen are eternal" (II Corinthians 4:16-18).

Adelaide continues to share with me her thoughts that fall right in line with the things I'm going through every day.

She expressed her thanks to Abba, the Father, for spiritual words of encouragement as she looked in the mirror and saw her body sagging and wrinkling.

Even as we feel the aches and pains, even as our steps are unsure, inside we dance with delight and joy. Inside where we live and have being, we soar with the eagles and take delight in our friendship with the Lord. Inside this body, we are being renewed and strengthened through Jesus' love and kindness.

Prayer

I need some help, Lord.

Today my spirit isn't soaring. Today my eyes have drifted from You to all the trials that surround me. Holy Spirit, who lives with me and within me, let me feel Your presence. God sent You to be my comforter. Help me feel the loving arms of God wrapped around me. Tuck me under Your protective wing. Let me rest and awaken refreshed, recharged, and ready to live in the peace and joy of Your presence.

Rejoice!

You are the children of the Kingdom of God.
You're the chosen ones for whom the Savior
came.
You're His noble creation by the Spirit and the
blood,
You're the church that He has built to bear His
name.
And the gates of hell shall not prevail against
you!
And the hordes of darkness cannot quench your
light;
And the host of God shall stand and fight beside
you,
'Till your King shall reign triumphant in His
might! [x]

Jimmy and Carol Owen

Prayer

Dear Lord, thank You for the words in this short poem by Jimmy and Carol Owen. They are on a yellowing piece of paper, torn from a larger piece, in my top drawer, and have been there for many years. I brought the paper home from somewhere—church, camp, I don't remember.

The words remind me of who I am. I look at them frequently because the world wants me to forget who I am. You, Lord, have given me this reminder taken from the scriptures. Help me always remember who I am and let me live my life as a child of the King.

Depression

A line by Charles Dickens (1812-1870) in *Oliver Twist* makes me laugh when I am having a pity-party: "'Come, Oliver! Wipe your eyes with the cuffs of your jacket, and don't cry into your gruel; that's a very foolish action, Oliver.'" [xi]

Sometimes I recognize the foolishness, when surrounded by all my blessings, I am distressed over some minor thing that I know better than to waste time being distressed about. But depression may also be overwhelming and debilitating. Sadly, Christians are not immune to severe depression and may feel guilty because they struggle with emotional trials.

In *The Pilgrim's Progress* by John Bunyan (1628-1688), "Christian was left to tumble in the Slough of Despond alone, but still he endeavored to struggle to that side of the slough that was farthest from his own house, and next to the wicket gate: which he did, but could not get out because of the burden on his back." [xii]

Sometimes we feel trapped in our worry, guilt, failures, or loneliness.

The scriptures say, *"Call to Me, and I will answer you, and will tell you great and hidden things, that you have not known"* (Jeremiah 33:3). Calling out to God is never a mistake—call and call and call. *"You will seek Me and find Me, when you seek for Me with your heart"* (Jeremiah 29:13).

However, initially in the two episodes in my life when I believe I was experiencing serious depression, reading scripture and praying seemed too hard to do. I felt stuck in my own mud pit. Yet, when I had no inclination to read or pray, it came to me that my children needed me, and I felt God say, *"Just give Me your hand and I will help you get up."* And He did.

As I began writing this devotional I considered what John Bunyan's Christian and I had in common as we struggled to escape the depression pit. There were a couple of things: Christian was told there were steps in the pit he could have used, but admittedly they were hard to see; and, a person named Help pulled Christian out of the pit.

My "Help" was a therapist. For others, help may come from a friend, a pastor or priest, or a psychiatrist. When depressed, look for and be willing to accept help.

When I found my steps, they included journaling my thoughts and including scriptures, poems, and the words of songs that encouraged me. Do your best to find your steps. Take those steps even if it's hard to do. They may include professional therapies and prescribed medication(s). Consider writing down and rereading words that minister to you.

As I worked on my steps, God worked on me. He taught me a great deal about forgiveness, forgiving others and forgiving myself. He taught me that His word is a soothing and healing balm. He taught me to wait as patiently as possible for my healing.

Trust and obey. When we do that, we learn that He is a miracle-working God, who not only heals, He restores and makes new. He has promised, *"I will never leave you nor forsake you"* (Hebrews 13:5b). And again, *"By his wounds you have been healed"* (I Peter 2:24).

In a later portion of his journey, Christian is captured by the Giant Despair. This time, the calming words of Christian's companion, Hopeful, encourage him to remember what God has brought him through and to remember God's promises. Christian has found the key to freedom. [xiii]

I waited patiently on the Lord;
He turned to me and heard my cry.
He lifted me out of the slimy pit,
Out of the mud and mire;
He set my feet on a rock
And gave me a firm place to stand.
He put a new song in my mouth,
A hymn of praise to our God.

Psalm 40: 1-3 (NIV)

Prayer

Heavenly Father, life is full of injustice and suffering. My earthly father would say, "If you aren't a little depressed, there is something wrong with you."

Jesus had a tender heart. He loved and healed the sick, the lame, and the blind, whether tax collector, prostitute, or a rich young ruler.

Thank You, Father, that in this lost and confused world You show us love, laughter, fun, beauty, music. They flow like a cool rain on a hot, dry land. Your rain pours down on the good and the bad. Help Your children notice the Good Samaritan, the brilliant doctor, the tender mother, the food-bank volunteer, the donated money, the baby kitten, the bud about to burst open into a leaf or a flower, the kind word, the words of wisdom and correction, the smile, and the rainbow. Help Your children remember these things are messages of love from You. I pray in the name of Your greatest gift, Jesus.

Loss of a Spouse

On average women live longer than men. In fact, 57% of all those ages 65 and older are women. By age 85, 67% are women. The average lifespan is about 5 years longer for women in the US, and about 7 years longer worldwide." [xiv] Many older women have lost or will lose a spouse.

With that loss come serious life changes. Whatever the relationship, the work of two will fall on one. The decisions of two become decisions made by one. There may be serious financial consequences, especially for couples who live primarily on their Social Security.

There is loneliness. Friends who have become widows after many years of marriage, tell me that losing a mate feels as if you have lost half of yourself.

God does not overlook the plight of the widow: *"...He upholds the widow..."* (Psalm 146:9), and the church is instructed that, *"Pure and undefiled religion before God, the Father is to visit...widows in their troubles"* (James 1:27, NKJV).

Scripture says, *"Elijah went up by a whirlwind into heaven. And Elisha...saw him no more"* (II Kings 2: 11-12, NKJV). Elisha was losing Elijah, who was his mentor; who had led him along the path to becoming a prophet; and, whom he called Father.

The Lord let Elisha grieve and then Elisha *"took the cloak of Elijah that had fallen from him"* (II Kings 2:12-13). Going it alone, taking the initiative, trusting God is what a woman who has lost her husband must do. God gave courage and strength to Elisha to fill Elijah's shoes. God will provide courage and strength for the widow who calls on Him. He has promised that she will not be alone: *"For your Maker is your husband, the Lord of Hosts is His name; and your Redeemer is the Holy One of Israel; He is called the God of the whole earth"* (Isaiah 54:5, NKJV).

Prayer

Dear Lord, "You are my hiding place; you shall preserve me from trouble: You shall surround me with songs of deliverance" (Psalm 32:7, NKJV).

I will "... hold fast the confession of our hope without wavering, for He who promised is faithful" (Hebrews 10:23).

Shadow to Light—Death to Life

"Precious [and of great consequence] in the sight of the Lord is the death of His Godly ones [so He watches over them]" (Psalm 116:15 AMP).

David
"When David's time to die drew near, he commanded Solomon his son, saying: I am about to go the way of all the earth..." (I Kings 2:1-2).

"What man can live and not see death? Can he deliver his life from the power of the grave?" (Psalm 89:48, NKJV).

"Even though I walk through the valley of the shadow of death, I will fear no evil; for you are with me..." (Psalm 23:4).

Isaiah
"The people who walked in darkness have seen a great light; those who dwelt in a land of deep darkness, on them, a light has shined" (Isaiah 9:2).

"He will swallow up death forever, And the Lord will wipe away tears from all faces; the reproach of his people he will take away for all the earth; for the Lord has spoken" (Isaiah 25:8).

"...because he poured out his soul to death, and He was numbered with the transgressors, yet He bore the sin of many..." (Isaiah 53:12b).

Paul

"...so that as sin reigned in death, grace also might reign through righteousness leading to eternal life through Jesus Christ our Lord" (Romans 5:21).

"For the wages of sin is death, but the free gift of God is eternal life in Christ Jesus our Lord" (Roman 6:23).

"For the law of the Spirit of life has set you free in Christ Jesus from the law of sin and death" (Romans 8:2).

"The last enemy to be destroyed is death" (I Corinthians 15:26).

"Death is swallowed up in victory" (I Corinthians 15:54b).

Praise God! And, *"...our Savior Jesus Christ, who abolished death and brought life and immortality to light through the gospel"* (II Timothy 1:10).

Prayer

Oh, how grateful I am, Lord.

*Thank You that I was born in this time and place.
Thank You that Your word is available written in
modern English, word- for-word or paraphrased.
Thank You that You, by the work of the Holy
Spirit through men and women, have explained the
plan.*

*Thank You for the printing press, for language
experts, and for translators who have changed Your
word from documents few could read to words
translated for every tribe and nation.*

*Thank You for David who met You as he tended
sheep, and experienced Your protection and love.
Thank You for Your Prophet Isaiah, who spoke of
what was to come. Thank You for Paul who met
Jesus on the road to Damascus and spoke with the
Apostles. Thank You that Your word shows us how
death was changed to life.*

How Firm a Foundation

A huge rock is located in Georgia. Stone Mountain is the largest piece of exposed granite in the world. What is above the earth is only the tip of the iceberg. It extends underground through much of north Georgia. Many houses are built upon that rock.

How firm a foundation, ye saints of the Lord,
Is laid for your faith in His excellent Word!
What more can He say than to you He hath
said,
To you who for refuge to Jesus have fled?

"Fear not! I am with thee; O be not dismayed,
For I am thy God. I will still give thee aid.
I'll strengthen thee, help thee,
And cause thee to stand,
Upheld by My righteous, omnipotent hand.

"When through fiery trials thy pathway shall lie,
My grace, all-sufficient, shall be thy supply.
The flames shall not hurt thee, I only design
Thy dross to consume and thy gold to refine.

"The soul that on Jesus hath leaned for repose;
I will not, I will not desert to his foes.
That soul, though all hell should endeavor to
shake,
I'll never, no never, no never forsake!"

Attributed to Keen (1787)

Prayer

My God and my Rock, we describe Your power and strength when we call You a Rock. You are the foundation that lasts through eternity. You are the foundation that is secure. Your laws never change. Your wisdom is perfect. Your guidance always correct. Let me stand, walk, and live on Your firm foundation.

Fear

It is wise to have some fear. We teach our children to be cautious of a hot stove, of boiling water, and of a busy street. We desire for them to develop a healthy fear of being burned or injured. The scriptures tell us to fear God: *"Oh that they had such a heart as this, always to fear Me and to keep all My commandments that it might go well with them and with their descendants forever!"* (Deuteronomy 5:29).

But, scriptures also warn us not to fear: *"You shall not fear them, for it is the Lord your God who fights for you"* (Deuteronomy 3:22).

Fear, with the accompanying adrenaline, may produce lifesaving fight or flight. Nevertheless, as a constant companion, it can produce serious physical and emotional illness.

Fear increases our desire to control other people and situations we perceive as threatening. Feelings of vulnerability may produce excessive action or paralysis. Many times, we fear emotional pain more than physical pain. We don't want our feelings hurt or to look foolish.

Fear may make us judgmental. There is wisdom in taking care of yourself, but the devil has a way of twisting good choices into compulsions, arrogance, and self-centeredness. We allow ourselves to think that a person who is poor, who is robbed, or who is ill, brought it on themselves. The temptation is to believe that if we avoid their mistake we will be safe.

Fear steals our peace, our trust, and our joy. Feelings of helplessness and hopelessness (depression) may follow.

There are many things in life that are beyond our control; but those things are not beyond God's control: *"I have said these things to you, that in Me you may have peace. In the world you will have tribulation; but take heart, I have overcome the world"* (John 16:33).

The greatest defense against fear is understanding the enormity of God's love. *"God is love"* (I John 4:16).

Packer writes: "So, the love of God who is Spirit is no fitful, fluctuating thing, as human love is, nor is it a mere impotent longing for things that may never be; it is, rather, a spontaneous determination of God's whole being in an attitude of benevolence and benefaction, an attitude freely chosen and firmly fixed." [xv]

Our God, who has made us, redeemed us, and who is sanctifying us, has chosen to love us eternally. We are God's. We were bought at a huge price, a *"purchased possession"* (Ephesians 1:14B, NKJV). Everything that comes into our lives is for his purpose and our good.

Just think of it: *"For I, the Lord your God, hold your right hand; it is I who says to you, 'Fear not, I am the one who helps you"* (Isaiah 41:12).

The Psalmist says to God, *"You hem me in, behind and before, and lay your hand upon me. Such knowledge is too wonderful for me: It is high, I cannot attain it"* (Psalm 139:5-6).

I am hemmed front and back by God, and fellow Christians are marching beside me.

God, *"You-Are-The-God-Who-Sees"* (Genesis 16: 13, NKJV) me.

"...God heard their groaning..." (Exodus 2:24), and he hears mine. *"As the mountains surround Jerusalem, so the Lord surrounds His people from this time forth and forever"* (Psalm 125:2). *"You surround me with songs of deliverance"* (Psalm 32:7b, NKJV).

Elisha and his servant awoke to find an Army had surrounded the city, and his servant said, *"Alas, my master! 'What shall we do?' So he answered, 'Do not be afraid, for those who are with us are more than those who are with them.' Then Elisha prayed and said, 'Lord, please open his eyes that he may see.' So the Lord opened the eyes of the young man, and he saw, and behold, the mountain was full of horses and chariots of fire all around Elisha"* (II Kings 6:15b-17).

"...God has not given us a spirit of fear, but of power and of love and of a sound mind" (II Timothy 1:7, NKJV).

Prayer

*Loving Father, one of the first Bible verses my
children ever learned was, "God has not given me a
spirit of fear, but of power and love and a sound
mind." I bring that verse as a prayer to you for my
children, grandchildren, and all my descendants.*

*In the changing world with all its complexities and
its ever-growing challenges, give them Godly
courage, confidence, and wisdom. Help them trust
in Your power and strength.*

Rock of Ages, Cleft for Me

Rock of Ages cleft for me,
Let me hide myself in Thee;
Let the water and the blood,
From Thy wounded side which flowed,
Be of sin the double cure,
Save from wrath and make me pure.

While I draw this final breath,
When my eyes shall close in death,
When I rise to worlds unknown
And behold Thee on Thy throne,
Rock of Ages, cleft for me,
Let me hide myself in Thee.

Augustus M. Toplady
(1740-1778)

The Stoney Heart

"And I will give you a new heart, and a new spirit I will put within you: I will remove the heart of stone from your flesh and give you a heart of flesh" (Ezekiel 36:26).

Once again, my friend Adelaide Beall brought me words that perfectly explained this passage. She told me this story:

There once was a little girl who was very sad. She never smiled. She felt so all alone. "What's the matter, my darling?" her mother asked. "You look so unhappy."

"Oh, mother," the child confessed, "I want friends, but I don't know how to make friends. I don't know how to love. My heart feels as heavy as a stone."

Her mother responded, "There is a secret that I will share with you. The way to love is to practice loving. Just as you practice riding your bike to learn to ride, or practice the piano to play, you must practice loving to love.

"Love is not a feeling but a commitment, a choice—a choice to be loving. Practice loving, my daughter, and see what happens."

And the little girl did. She practiced loving. She smiled at people. She was helpful to others. She chose to be joyful instead of sad. She practiced hugging. She made a commitment to love.

Then a miracle happened! Instead of the old heart of stone, she had a heart that was filled with joy, compassion, mercy and love. She had been given a new heart...a heart just like her mother described.

Prayer

*Lord Jesus, You who called the children to come
to You, who reached out to heal, who taught
fishermen to save souls, who longed to gather those
who hated Him to Himself as a mother hen gathers
her chicks under her wings, make me like You.
Make my heart generous toward others. Help me
be generous as You have been generous to me.
Help me forgive as You have forgiven me. Help
me be useful to You by loving as You have loved
me. Let me reflect Your love in this world. Like the
moon reflects the sun, let my life reflect the Son.*

Chronic Pain, Illness, and Disability

Many of us are introduced to chronic pain, illness, and disability as we grow older. Pain that is constant is entirely different than acute pain. Illness that leads to disability comes with complexities and has potential for many complications. Ongoing pain and debilitating illness may seem impossible to endure. Paul shares his discouragement with longstanding disability in II Corinthians 12:8: *"Three times I pleaded with the Lord that it should leave me."*

Job cried, *"Where then is my hope?"* (Job 17:15, NKJV).

I have been a nurse a long time, and I have seen people dealing with pain and disability with varying degrees of success. Some are astounding. There is the joyful face of a little child who just went through a chemotherapy infusion, or a soldier missing limbs competing on "Dancing with the Stars." There is also the denial of a diabetic young person, who eventually loses his sight and the feeling in his legs, because he won't eat correctly or pay attention to his insulin.

What I do know is that in my life, and in the testimony of innumerable Christians, God meets every need of His children. Whatever comes, our God is there. He responded to Paul, *"My grace is sufficient for you, for My power is made perfect in weakness"* (II Corinthians 12:9). Paul responds, *"Therefore, for the sake of Christ, I am content with* weakness, insults, hardships, persecutions, and calamities. For when I am weak, then I am strong" (II Corinthians 12:10).

We as Christians also find that suffering is something we share in a mysterious way with Christ. He suffered for us, and as we suffer we are closer to Him. Paul calls it the fellowship of his suffering: *"...that I may know Him and the power of His resurrection, and may share His suffering, becoming like Him in His death..."* (Philippians 3:10).

"My health may fail, and my spirit may grow weak, but God remains the strength of my heart; He is mine forever" (Psalm 73:26 NLT).

"There is none like God, O Jeshurun, who rides through the heavens to Your help, Through the skies in His majesty. The eternal God is your dwelling place, and underneath are the everlasting arms, and He thrust out the enemy before you and said, 'Destroy!'" (Deuteronomy 33: 26-27).

Prayer

Help me, Lord! I need You to do something! Heal me, decrease the pain, distract me, or tell me how to accept and live with this pain. Right now, it's agony. If I need to learn something, help me learn and be done with it. If somehow my pain will help others, give me the willingness to bear it for others. Help me to love that much; help me to love like You love.

I count on You to show me how to live my life to the fullest. Help me to laugh, sing, and love, while carrying the cross You have given me to bear.

Plans While in Prison

The most important part of our task will be to tell everyone who will listen that Jesus is the only answer to the problems that are disturbing the hearts of men and nations. We shall have the right to speak because we can tell from our experience that His light is more powerful than the deepest darkness...How wonderful that the reality of His presence is greater than the reality of the hell about us.[xvi]

From Betsie ten Boon,
to her sister Corrie

Betsie died Dec. 16, 1944 at the age of 59, during her stay at Ravensbrück, a women's concentration camp.

Giving

"Jesus looked up and saw the rich putting their gifts into the offering box, and He saw a poor widow put in two small copper coins. And He said, 'Truly, I tell you, this poor widow has put in more than all of them. For they all contributed out of their abundance, but she out of her poverty put in all she had to live on'" (Luke 21: 1-4).

The Lord has been generous in the friends He has given me. Virginia Smith, a sister in my church family, shared her story with me on how she learned firsthand how important it is to first give to the Lord.

Life over 50 can be hard financially. Corporate America has decided employees over the age of 50 are a liability rather than an asset. In our fathers' generation, employee loyalty was rewarded with some degree of financial security—health benefits, pension, paid time off. Not so in our generation. Never had Virginia's faith been tested more than in the past 10 years. And never had she trusted God more.

She and her husband decided to tithe about the time things got hard. Her husband is a salesman. When the housing market went bust, so did the market that her dearly-beloved sold to. His job, like so many others, was a casualty of the Great Recession. He was 51—not a prime prospect for the sales positions out there. He was too old to be hired, too young to collect on retirement benefits, therein lies the catch 22.

The Lord decided to test their faith during this time. They made an important decision—if they had a paycheck, the church got the first 10 percent.

You've probably heard the story about a millionaire who would stoop down and pick up pennies when he found them on the street. When questioned why a man of such wealth would bother with a penny he would say, "It reminds me who I put my trust in. It is stamped on the penny, 'In God We Trust', and it reminds me that God is in control and we are to trust Him."

It's no coincidence that during their most difficult times, Virginia and her husband found pennies wherever they went, but especially at the church. They found them in the parking lot, on the sidewalk, in the church, and in the student center. Every time, they picked them up and thanked God that He is in control. It is a tangible reminder that we are to trust Him, no matter the circumstances.

The parallel between the pennies and the two small copper coins in Luke's account of the parable of the widow's offering is unmistakable. They are both copper, obviously, but they also represent giving when the instinct is to withhold.

You cannot receive when your fist is tightly clamped around something you should give.

So my friends gave. And in turn, they received. The Lord has been very faithful to them. They were able to meet their obligations. The household accounting doesn't make sense—they shouldn't be able to do what they did with what they had, but somehow the Lord made it work.

So whether it's the widow's offering or pennies from heaven, give to the Lord and His work, trust Him, and He will reward you for your faithfulness!

Prayer

Lord, make me a giver. I want to experience the miracle. How does one give away and end up with more and not less? It makes no mathematical sense.

You tell us in Malachi 3:10 to test You on this issue. "Bring the full tithe into the storehouse, that there may be food in My house. And thereby put Me to the test, says the Lord of Hosts, if I will not open the windows of heaven for you and pour down for you a blessing until there is no more need."

Anger and Bitterness

"Woe to him who strives with his Maker!" (Isaiah 45:9a, NKJV).

Common emotions related to loss may recur randomly within the normal grieving process. However, getting stuck in any stage may be problematic. Anger may become debilitating. When anger remains for years, bitterness may grow and may destroy a person's ability to experience any peace or any joy.

Peter, speaking to the Sorcerer, said, *"Repent therefore of your wickedness, and pray God if perhaps the thought of your heart may be forgiven you. For I see you are poisoned by bitterness..."* (Acts 8:22-23a, NKJV).

The antidote to this poison is trusting God, trusting His love for you, and trusting His purposes in your life and the lives of others. Jeremiah proclaims, *"Blessed is the man who trusts in the Lord and whose hope is the Lord. For he shall be like a tree planted by the water, which spreads its roots by the river, and will not fear when the heat comes; but its leaf will be green, and will not be anxious in a year of drought, nor will cease from yielding fruit"* (Jeremiah 17:7-8, NKJV).

God is telling us that after a tragedy that brings great pain, there can be new life. Roots dug deep will survive heat and drought. Shallow roots, as described in the parable of the sower, burn up: *"And when the sun rose, it was scorched, and since it had no root, it withered away"* (Mark 4:6).

Dig deep into the word of God. Ask the Holy Spirit to lead you through emotional healing, and to teach you about God's infinite love.

"Cease from anger and forsake wrath: Do not fret—it only causes harm" (Psalm 37:8 NKJV).

"Do not be overcome by evil, but overcome evil with good" (Romans 12:21 NIV).

"...those who plan peace have joy" (Proverbs 12:20b).

Prayer

Lord, here I am again. I am on my knees at Your feet saying I am willing to forgive. I want to be free of this anger. I don't want to feel bitter any more.

Nevertheless, I can't do it. I can't seem to escape these feelings. You will have to fix this, Lord. You must make it happen.

Here I am, bringing it to You. I am giving it to You, willing to let it go. Help me not to take it back.

Thank You in advance for setting me free. Thank You in advance for returning my joy, my peace, and my trust. So be it!

Mercy

In *Daily Prayers for Use in Families,* inside *An Anglican Prayer Book,* the morning prayers start: "New are Your mercies each morning, Lord, and great is Your faithfulness."[xvii] Another prayer begins, "Gracious Father, we recognize that it is by Your mercy that another day is added to our lives." [xviii] Where would I be without God's mercy?

God expects me to follow Him in showing mercy: *"He has shown you, O man, what is good; and, what does the Lord require of you but to do justly, to love mercy, and to walk humbly with your God"* (Micah 6:8, NKJV).

"Blessed are the merciful..." (Matthew 5:7).

My lack of mercy shows when I judge, when I refuse to forgive, and when I gossip.

Our Lord tells me to, *"Judge not, that you be not judged. For with the judgment you pronounce you will be judged, and with the measure you use it will be measured to you. Why do you see the speck that is in your brother's eye, but do not notice the log that is in your own eye?"* (Luke 6:32).

The Lord also says, *"For if you forgive others their trespasses, your heavenly Father will also forgive you, but if you do not forgive others their trespasses, neither will your Father forgive your trespasses"* (Matthew 6:14-15).

Finally, gossip appears in Paul's comprehensive list of sins, right between maliciousness and slanderers (Romans 1:29-30).

James 3:17 says, *"But the wisdom that is from above is first pure, then peaceable, gentle, willing to yield, full of mercy and good fruits, without partiality and without hypocrisy"* (NKJV).

Prayer

*Dear Lord, help me remove the "they deserve
that" from my thoughts. What do I know about it?
Make me keenly aware of how little I know about
the lives of others. Give me a tender and gentle
spirit. Help me to build up and not to tear down.
Help me to err toward kindness.*

The Merchant of Venice, Act IV, Scene I

The quality of mercy is not strained;
It droppeth as the gentle rain from heaven
Upon the place beneath. It is twice blest;
It blesseth him that gives and him that takes:
'Tis mightiest in the mightiest; it becomes
The throned monarch better than his crown:
His sceptre shows the force of temporal power,
The attribute to awe and majesty,
Wherein doth sit the dread and fear of kings;
But mercy is above this sceptered sway;
It is enthroned in the hearts of kings,

It is an attribute to God himself;
And earthly power doth then show likest God's
When mercy seasons justice.

William Shakespeare
(1564-1616)

Guilt

James tells us, *"For whoever shall keep the whole law, but fails in one point, has become guilty of all"* (2:10). Most of us cannot say, "Oh, shoot! Only one sin and I'm out." Our sins are many. I am sometimes embarrassed before God, as I return again and again asking forgiveness for repeating the same sin.

Not only do we sin, but we were born into the sinful human condition. *"Behold, I was brought forth in iniquity, and in sin did my mother conceive me"* (Psalm 51:5).

Sin is not only an action on our part that may hurt another person, the earth, or the Church. Sin is rebellion against God. David said, *"Against You, You only have I sinned and done what is evil in Your sight, so that You may be justified in Your words and blameless in Your judgment"* (Psalm 51:4). Sin is always rebellion against God. Through the sacrifice of animals, God taught us that sin leads to death; and, that there are always consequences for sin. There is no victimless crime.

Only God could solve our desperate sin problem. He (God the Son) came from glory, and paid the price for our sin. *"For God so loved the world, that He gave His only Son, that whoever believes in Him should not perish but have eternal life. For God did not send His Son into the world to condemn the world, but in order that the world might be saved through Him"* (John 3:16-17).

Jesus removed the ultimate consequence—eternal separation from God. God completely forgives those who call on Him for forgiveness because of the sacrificial work of Jesus. Fellowship between God and mankind is restored. *"There is therefore now no condemnation to those who are in Christ Jesus"* (Romans 8:1, NKJV). How wondrous! *"...as far as the east is from the west, so far does He remove our transgressions from us"* (Psalm 103:12).

"This God is my strong refuge and has made my way blameless" (II Samuel 22:33).

Prayer

Thank You, thank You, thank You, Lord.

And Can It Be That I Should Gain?

And can it be that I should gain
An interest in the Savior's blood?
Died He for me who caused His pain?
For me who Him to death pursued?
Amazing love! How can it be
That Thou my God, shouldst die for me?

He left His Father's throne above,
So free, so infinite His grace!
Emptied Himself of all but love,
And bled for Adam's helpless race!
Tis mercy all immense and free,
For O my God, it found out me.

Long my imprisoned spirit lay
Fast bound in sin and nature's night.
Thine eye diffused a quickening ray;
I woke—the dungeon flamed with light!
My chains fell off, my heart was free,
I rose went forth and followed Thee.

No condemnation now I dread:
Jesus, and all in Him is mine!
Alive in Him, my living Head,
And clothed in righteousness divine,
Bold I approach the eternal throne,
And claim the crown, through Christ my own.

Charles Wesley
(1707-1788)

Healing Prayer

Shirley Hauser is a member of the Upper Room Chapter of the Daughters of the Holy Cross and a great source of inspiration to me. This is her account of her own divine healing.

Shirley had been a prayer warrior for a long time and had seen God heal many people.

Her ankle started to hurt a few years ago. She went to the doctor, and he told her that her Achilles tendon was sprained and sent her to physical therapy. After weeks of therapy, her ankle was no better. Next was an MRI, which showed a tear in the tendon. She was facing surgery and an eight-week period to recuperate.

We were having the Maundy Thursday service at church, and it included the foot washing ceremony. As she sat in the pew, Shirley heard God tell her, "Go get your foot washed."

Shirley doesn't like anyone touching her feet, so she just sat there. Again, she heard His instruction. So, she gave in and went up front to have her feet washed. Nothing miraculous happened, so she limped back to her seat.

The next morning, she got up, and the pain was gone! Praise God!

God is still in the miracle business. We just need to ask. He is the Great Physician.

He does heal, sometimes not in the way we expect. But, His way is always the right way. If it's His will, it will happen in His time.

The scripture says, *"Is any one of you sick? He should call the elders of the church to pray over him and anoint him with oil in the name of the Lord. And the prayer offered in faith will make the sick person well; the Lord will raise him up"* (James 5:13-15 NIV).

Prayer

Lord, I pray for healing. Make me well. Give me a healthy body and a healthy mind. Heal my soul. If I need more faith, give me more faith.

Send a healer. Speak the words, "Be healed," over me, and I will be healed.

Let me touch the hem of your garment, or reach out and touch me. I pray in the name of Him who heals the sick.

Speaking of Foot-Washing

If you are a mom, you have washed a lot of feet. If you are caring for a sick or elderly family member, feet are just part of it. If you are a nurse, you have lost count of the feet you have seen and cleaned.

Washing feet is no big deal, but letting someone else wash your feet is a whole different matter. Remember Peter's reaction to Jesus washing his feet: *"You shall never wash my feet!"* (John 13:8).

We don't mind so much if we are paying someone to give us a pedicure, or even if it is the nurse paid to care for us. But what about a friend or a stranger? Truth-be-told, feet are very personal things. They may be ticklish, and they may stink. They may have funny-looking middle toes that are longer that the big toes—like mine. Why do feet bother us so much? Is it pride? Maybe so.

As we age there is a good chance we must swallow lots of pride. There will be many personal things with which we need help—dressing, eating, walking, driving, bill paying, and things we haven't yet considered. Things we have done for ourselves all these years—will we do them until we die? I hope so, but chances are slim that we will.

We understand God's asking us to die to self and live for Him. Maybe the last great opportunity to become more like Christ will be the humility of needing help and accepting it from those God sends to provide it.

In John 21, Jesus is talking to Peter about feeding his sheep. Then He makes a statement that is explained in verse 19: *"This He said to show by what kind of death He was to glorify God."*

Jesus says, *"Truly, truly I say to you, when you were young, you used to dress yourself and walked wherever you wanted; but when you are old, you will stretch out your hands, and another will dress you and carry you where you do not want to go"* (John 21:18).

This may be the time when it will be the hardest to say yes. Say yes when God says, *"Humble yourselves therefore under the mighty hand of God so that in the proper time He may exalt you, casting all your anxieties on Him, because He cares for you"* (I Peter 5:6-7).

> Lord, my heart is not proud,
> Lord my eyes are not haughty.
> I do not concern myself with great matters
> Or things too wonderful for me.
> But, I have calmed and quieted myself,
> I am like a weaned child with its mother;
> Like a weaned child, I am content.
> Psalm 131: 1-2 (NIV)

Prayer

Yes, Lord, I will go. I will go where You send me. Take my hand as You promised and walk with me. Station an angel at my bedside and one to guard my door. Let only those sent by You enter. Help me trust Your faithfulness. (The rudest doctor may be a genius.) Let me rest in Your arms, safe and secure.

Strength

My friend Virginia Smith shared her thoughts about strength with me.

The word strength conjures up visions of muscle-bound weight lifters and commercials for paper towels. As we age, we find our muscles and physical strength failing us year-by-year. Some resort to exercise to help maintain their strength with gym memberships, yoga, Zumba. We find that if we don't move, we may become unable to move. Arthritis and other chronic conditions complicate the matter further. Some choose to do nothing and succumb to the gradual decay of muscles and joints.

In Virginia's observation of people over the years, there is a distinct difference between those who move and those who don't. The movers live longer and are on fewer medications for major chronic illness such as diabetes and hypertension.

Let's consider a different kind of strength. Everyone has that strong person in their life. It may be a family member, a coworker, a friend. You know them. They are the person who remains unflappable in the face of adversity. They are the go-to person when life gets messy.

Where do they get their strength? Are they strong in the Lord or are they strong in themselves?

Virginia once had someone tell her, "Virginia, you're the strongest woman I know!" At the time, she took it as a compliment, while sensing her life was falling apart around her.

She thought she was in control of things. From the outside, her life looked great—she had been married to Steve for 20 years. She had two handsome sons. Virginia had a management-level position at work and was active in ministry at our church. They had money, a nice house in a nice neighborhood, and nice cars.

What people didn't know was that Virginia and her husband were drifting apart. They had a son who struggled with mental illness and was constantly in trouble at school. She worked for a boss from whom she never knew what to expect when she walked in the door to work.

Concerning that ministry at church, Virginia went through all the right motions, attended church faithfully, and put money in the plate. She claimed to be a Christian, had been raised in the Church, and was confirmed when she was ten. But she was doubting whether she knew Jesus. Maybe a little. Did she know the Holy Spirit? Definitely not. She was raised in a culture where the Holy Spirit was acclaimed in the Creeds, but not acknowledged in our lives.

Then she discovered that is where real strength comes from! The power of the Holy Spirit strengthens us when we let Him. When we put our trust in God, the Holy Spirit gives us the strength we need to face all adversities. As Paul stated in his Epistle to the Philippians in 4:13, *"I can do all things through him who strengthens me."* Wow! What a promise!

Virginia changed her priorities. She learned to trust that when you put God first in your life, everything else will fall into place. She thanks God every day that He is in control of her life now. She has taken herself off the throne of her life and placed Jesus there, and she found that He's a much better ruler than she is!

Prayer

You are my King. Lord, You are my Father.

When I am weakest, You are the strongest as You guard me. Show Your power to this child of Yours. Through the Holy Spirit, who Jesus promised would be my comforter, bring peace, joy, and rest. We will join the saints who praise You night and day. They gather around the throne of heaven.

Praise you, Lord, now and forever!

Acknowledgements

Bunyan, John, *The Pilgrim's Progress*, Grand Rapids, Michigan: Zondervan Publishing House, 1967.

Dickens, Charles, *Oliver Twist*, Mineola, NY: Dover Publications, Inc., 2002.

Lewis, C.S., *Letters to Malcolm*. copyright CS Lewis Pte Ltd, 1964. Extracts used with permission from First Mariner Books edition 2012.

Lewis, C.S., *Mere Christianity*. copyright CS Lewis Pte Ltd, 1942, 1943, 1944, 1953. Extracts used by permission from First Harper Collins paperback edition.

Owen, Jimmy and Carol, "Rejoice" from the musical, *Heal Our Land, 1995.*

Packer, J.I., *Knowing God.* Copyright 1973 by J. I. Packer. Extracts used with permission from InterVarsity Press, Downers Grove, IL.

Shmerling, Robert H., M.D., "Why men often die earlier than women," Harvard Heath, Feb. 19, 2016, www.health.harvard.edu/healthbeat.

Ten Boom, Corrie, *Amazing Love. Copyright* 1953 by Corrie ten Boom. Used by permission of CLC Publications. May not be further reproduced. All rights reserved.

An Anglican prayer Book, Contemporary English Services based on those in *The Book of Common Prayer and The Ordinal*, in their English 1662, American 1928, and Canadian

1962 editions. Preservation Press of the Prayer
Book Society of the U.S.A., published for The
Anglican Mission in America 2008.

The Book of Common Prayer, 1928, New York,
Oxford Press.

News Messenger (Blacksburg, VA), July 10, 2016.

Notes

[i] C.S. Lewis, *Letters to Malcolm*, copyright CS Lewis Pte Ltd, 1964. Extracts used with permission.

[ii] J.I. Packer, *Knowing God* (Downers Grove IL: Intervarsity Press, 1973), 123. Extracts used with permission.

[iii] CS Lewis, *Mere Christianity*, copyright CS Lewis Pte Ltd, 1942, 1943, 1944, 1953. Extracts used by permission, 86.

[iv] *An Anglican Prayer Book*, Contemporary English Services based on those in *The Book of Common Prayer and The Ordinal*, in their English 1662, American 1928, and Canadian 1962 editions. (Preservation Press of the Prayer Book Society of the U.S.A., published for The Anglican Mission in America 2008.), 158.

[v] *The Book of Common Prayer*, 1928, New York, Oxford Press, 342.

[vi] *News Messenger* (Blacksburg, VA), July 10, 2016.

[vii] Packer, 103.

[viii] Ibid., 90.

[ix] *An Anglican Prayer Book*, 168.

[x] Jimmy and Carol Owen, "Rejoice" from the musical, *Heal Our Land, 1995.*

[xi] Charles Dickens, *Oliver Twist,* Mineola, NY: Dover Publications, Inc., 2002, 16.

[xii] John Bunyan, *The Pilgrim's Progress*, Grand Rapids, Michigan: Zondervan Publishing House, 1967, 21.

[xiii] Ibid., 109, 110.

[xiv] Robert H. Shmerling, M.D., "Why men often die earlier than women," Harvard Heath, Feb. 19, 2016, www.health.harvard.edu/healthbeat.

[xv] J.I. Packer, *Knowing God*, 121.

[xvi] Corrie ten Boom, *Amazing Love*, Copyright 1953 by Corrie ten Boom. Used by permission of CLC Publications. May not be further reproduced. All rights reserved, 9.

[xvii] *An Anglican Prayer Book*, 165.

[xviii] Ibid., 168.

CPSIA information can be obtained
at www.ICGtesting.com
Printed in the USA
LVOW09*1208040518
575072LV00005B/3/P